R. Vaughan Williams

ROMANCE
for
Viola and Piano

Oxford University Press

ROMANCE
for Viola and Piano

The viola part edited by Bernard Shore
The piano part edited by Eric Gritton

R. VAUGHAN WILLIAMS

There is no information about the approximate date on which this work was written. The manuscript was discovered with others, without any clue, among the composer's papers after his death. All that can be said is that it was probably intended for the great virtuoso Lionel Tertis, for whom Vaughan Williams had composed his two major works for the viola — *Flos Campi* in 1925 and the Suite in 1934.

Bernard Shore

A separate viola part is included with this score

This work was first performed by Bernard Shore and Eric Gritton in a Macnaghten Concert on 19 January 1962

Romance

Poco animato

Viola

ROMANCE
for Viola and Piano

Edited by Bernard Shore

R. VAUGHAN WILLIAMS

There is no information about the approximate date on which this work was written. The manuscript was discovered with others, without any clue, among the composer's papers after his death. All that can be said is that it was probably intended for the great virtuoso Lionel Tertis, for whom Vaughan Williams had composed his two major works for the viola — *Flos Campi* in 1925 and the Suite in 1934.

Bernard Shore

This work was first performed by Bernard Shore and Eric Gritton in a Macnaghten Concert on 19 January 1962

Viola

Romance

OXFORD UNIVERSITY PRESS

Romance

Romance

OXFORD UNIVERSITY PRESS

OXFORD MUSIC FOR VIOLA includes:

Bach *arr. Forbes*	Sheep may safely graze
arr. Forbes	A first year classical album
	A second year classical album
	Baroque Pieces
	Classical and Romantic Pieces
	Popular Pieces
	Tunes and Dances
Handel *arr. Forbes*	The arrival of the Queen of Sheba
	Sonata in G
Mackay	Easy position tunes
	A modern viola method
Murray and Tate	The New Viola Books, Book 2
Vaughan Williams	Romance

ISBN 978-0-19-359271-1

OXFORD UNIVERSITY PRESS

9 780193 592711